NATURE'S LIGHT SHOW

SHOOTING STARS

By Kristen Rajczak

Gareth Stevens
Publishing

Please visit our website, www.garethstevens.com. For a free color catalog of all our high-quality books, call toll free 1-800-542-2595 or fax 1-877-542-2596.

Library of Congress Cataloging-in-Publication Data

Rajczak, Kristen.
Shooting stars / Kristen Rajczak.
    p. cm. — (Nature's light show)
Includes index.
ISBN 978-1-4339-7036-8 (pbk.)
ISBN 978-1-4339-7037-5 (6-pack)
ISBN 978-1-4339-7035-1 (library binding)
1. Meteors—Juvenile literature. I. Title.
QB741.5.R35 2013
523.5'1—dc23

                            2011045159

First Edition

Published in 2013 by
Gareth Stevens Publishing
111 East 14th Street, Suite 349
New York, NY 10003

Designer: Katelyn E. Reynolds
Editor: Kristen Rajczak

Photo credits: Cover, p. 1, (cover, pp. 1, 3–24 background) Jorge Guerrero/AFP/Getty Images; (cover, pp. 1, 3–24 graphics) Shutterstock.com; p. 4 Photos.com/Thinkstock; pp. 5, 13 Lodriguss Gerard/Photo Researchers/Getty Images; p. 8 John Mottern/AFP/Getty Images; p. 9 Howard Edin (Oklahoma City Astronomy Club)/NASA; p. 11 Edward Kinsman/Photo Researchers/Getty Images; pp. 12, 18 Jamal Nasrallah/AFP/Getty Images; p. 14 Stephen Shaver/AFP/Getty Images; p. 15 Ethan Miller/Getty Images; p. 17 Aura/NOAO/NSF/Getty Images; p. 19 Photo Researchers/Getty Images; p. 20 Blaine Franger/UpperCut Images/Getty Images; p. 21 Jerry Schad/Photo Researchers/Getty Images.

Printed in the United States of America

CPSIA compliance information: Batch #CS12GS: For further information contact Gareth Stevens, New York, New York at 1-800-542-2595.

CONTENTS

Words in the glossary appear in **bold** type the first time they are used in the text.

SEEING "STARS"

Seeing shooting stars flash across the night sky can be magical! Sometimes, they're called falling stars because they look like a star is "falling" right out of the sky. But did you know these beautiful lights aren't stars?

A shooting star is a **celestial** event called a meteor. People have observed and studied meteors for many years. However, meteors weren't known to be from space until the mid-1800s. Today, scientists know what causes shooting stars and even when to look for them!

Sometimes you can see many meteors at once.

"Meteor" and "meteorology" both come from a Greek word that means "high in the air." Meteorology is the study of Earth's **atmosphere** and weather.

Don't blink! Meteors commonly last less than a second.

5

WHAT'S A METEOR?

Each time a **comet** gets close to the sun, it melts and loses bits of itself. These bits are called meteoroids. They're made of rock and other planetary materials. A meteor is the streak of light caused by a meteoroid entering Earth's atmosphere.

Most meteors occur when Earth's **orbit** crosses the path of **debris** left by a comet's orbit. This path is called the meteoroid stream. Meteoroids from the stream move into Earth's atmosphere at high speeds.

EYE ON THE SKY

Some meteoroids come from asteroids, which are large chunks of rock and metallic material that travel around the solar system.

6

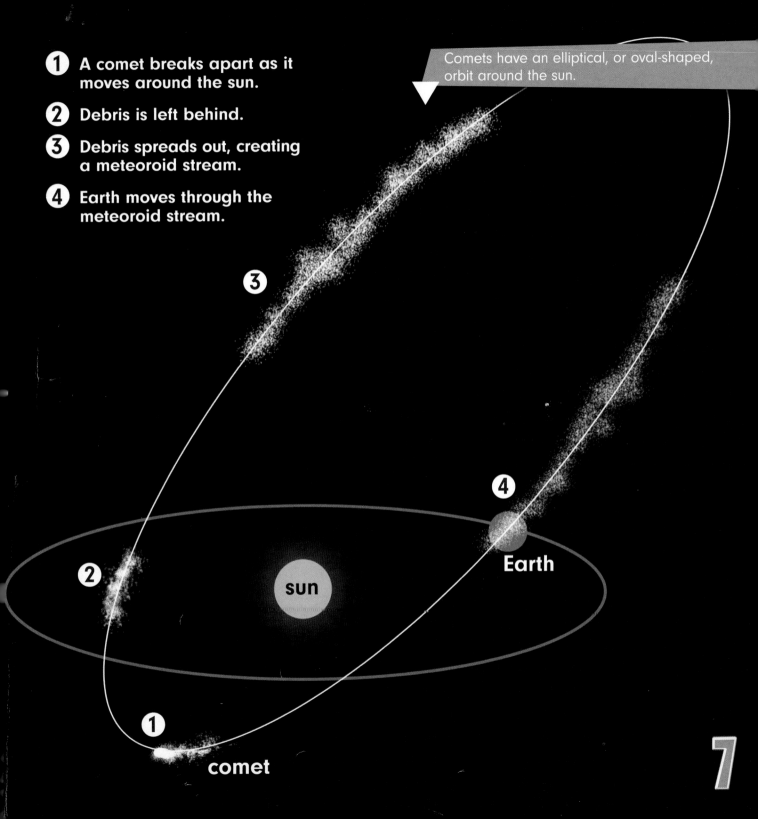

1. A comet breaks apart as it moves around the sun.

2. Debris is left behind.

3. Debris spreads out, creating a meteoroid stream.

4. Earth moves through the meteoroid stream.

Comets have an elliptical, or oval-shaped, orbit around the sun.

sun

Earth

comet

7

LIGHT UP!

When a meteoroid enters Earth's atmosphere, it has a lot of energy and speed. **Friction** with gas **molecules** causes it to slow down and heat up. The meteoroid loses some of its energy to the gas molecules. They release some of this energy as light, while the meteoroid glows and burns up. That's the light we see as a shooting star!

Most meteoroids that cause meteors are only about the size of a grain of sand. However, meteoroids can be many feet across.

A meteor's color comes from what it's made of and the gases it meets in the atmosphere.

Meteoroids may move as fast as 160,000 miles (257,440 km) per hour.

The streak of light that shows a meteor's path in the sky is called the meteor trail.

METEORITES

Some meteoroids fall to Earth! Meteoroids that reach Earth's surface are called meteorites, and they're nothing to be afraid of. The atmosphere is often able to break a large meteoroid into smaller bits and slow it down before it reaches the ground.

The outside of a meteorite melts when it enters Earth's atmosphere, but it doesn't burn up completely like most meteoroids. After it falls to Earth, a meteorite is cool enough to touch, though the outside will have been burned to a glossy black.

EYE ON THE SKY

Some meteorites come from the moon! These are called lunaites.

11

MANY METEORS

Earth sometimes passes through a part of space with a lot of comet debris. More meteoroids in space mean more meteors in our skies! This light show is called a meteor shower. Meteor showers often occur at the same time every year, when Earth's orbit crosses the comet's path again.

Have you ever seen shooting stars while camping? These are sporadic meteors. They are meteors that don't seem to be part of a shower. Most nights, meteors occur as often as every 10 or 15 minutes.

Meteors flash and shine over a desert in Jordan.

A meteor shower may last a few days, but its intensity, or strength, will change from day to day.

EYE ON THE SKY

A comet's orbit may take many years to complete, while Earth's orbit only takes a year. Earth passes through meteoroid streams that may have been created by a comet's orbit many years before.

ANNUAL METEOR SHOWERS

Some **annual** meteor showers have been observed for centuries. They're often named for the **constellation** they appear to come from. However, meteor showers don't really start at constellations! These names just help observers know where in the sky to look for a shower.

One of the most exciting yearly meteor showers happens in August. The Perseids commonly occur between July 25 and August 18. On an active night, you may see 50 to 100 meteors an hour!

This picture shows another annual meteor shower, the Leonids.

Meteors in a shower look to us like they're coming from the same spot in the sky. This is called the radiant point.

The Perseid meteor shower is named for the constellation Perseus.

15

METEOR STORMS

For about an hour on November 17, 1966, the Leonid meteor stream produced about 40 shooting stars each second! This was part of a meteor storm, an occurrence when meteors fall even more quickly and frequently than a meteor shower. In order to be called a storm, meteors must fall at a rate of 1,000 per hour or more.

Meteor storms are caused by Earth passing through a meteoroid stream with a lot of debris in it. Storms don't happen very often.

EYE ON THE SKY

A meteor outburst is an increase in meteor activity that may look like a meteor shower, but isn't formally part of one. Some outbursts may be minor meteor showers that just aren't well known.

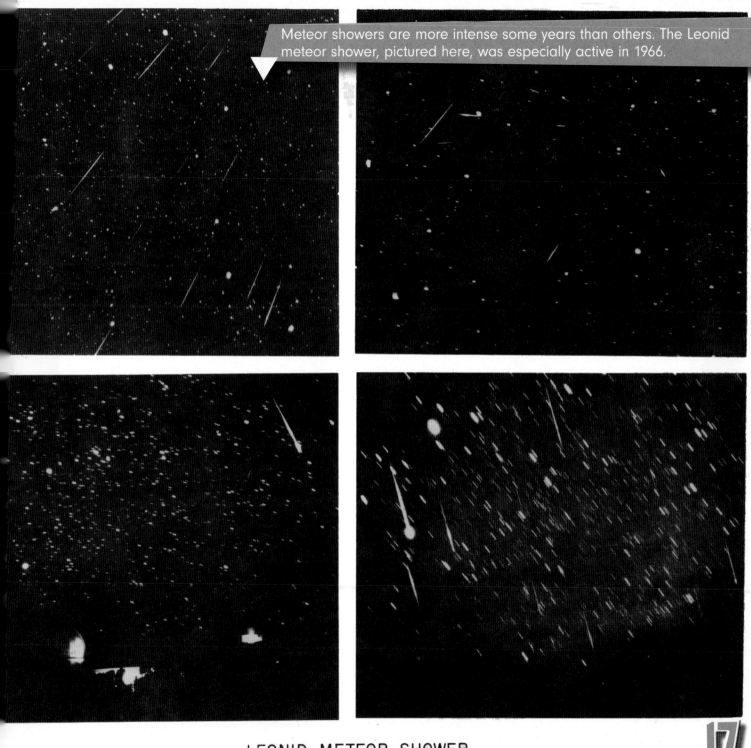

Meteor showers are more intense some years than others. The Leonid meteor shower, pictured here, was especially active in 1966.

LEONID METEOR SHOWER
NOV 18 1966 (AS SEEN FROM KITT PEAK)

WHEN TO WATCH

Meteors are most often seen just before sunrise. The leading edge of Earth, or the side experiencing morning, tends to run into more space debris than the trailing, or evening, edge.

Summer and fall are the best seasons to watch for shooting stars. In September, as many as 16 sporadic meteors could "fall" in an hour close to dawn! However, during the winter, fewer shooting stars are observed. By March, there might only be 4 to 8 seen near dawn.

Meteor showers are quite a sight!

Meteor shower activity can be seen better in the Northern **Hemisphere** than the Southern Hemisphere.

You may see twice as many shooting stars at dawn as during other parts of the night.

CATCH A FALLING STAR!

The most likely time to see a shooting star is during a meteor shower. It's fun to watch for them other nights, too!

When you hear about a meteor shower, plan to watch during the most active night of the shower. Meteor showers are commonly best seen between midnight and early morning. Find out where in the sky the shower will occur, so you can watch that area. Observe the shower away from lights if you can. Then, lie back and enjoy the show!

Some people camp out to see shooting stars!

STORIES ABOUT SHOOTING STARS

People all over the world have often wondered why stars "fall." Here are some common stories about shooting stars:

Some groups in East Africa believe shooting stars are gods appearing. Others believe they mean bad times are ahead.

The Native Americans thought shooting stars were the spirits of the dead or a warning that war was coming.

In ancient Persia, it was thought that shooting stars were witches that the star gods needed to fight.

Many people today believe if you see a shooting star, you should make a wish. Others think seeing a shooting star is lucky!

GLOSSARY

annual: returning every year

atmosphere: the gases surrounding Earth

celestial: having to do with the sky

comet: a celestial body that orbits in space and often forms a bright tail when near the sun

constellation: a grouping of stars that has been given a name and often has a story connected with it

debris: pieces of something that has been broken down

friction: the resistance of motion between two things

hemisphere: one of the halves of Earth. The equator divides Earth into the Northern and Southern Hemispheres.

molecule: one of the small bits that make up matter

orbit: to move in a set path around the sun. Also, the movement around the sun.

FOR MORE INFORMATION

Books

Atkinson, Stuart. *Comets, Asteroids, and Meteors.* Chicago, IL: Raintree Publishing, 2013.

Trammel, Howard K. *The Solar System.* New York, NY: Children's Press, 2010.

Young, Helen, and Chris Oxlade. *Weather and Space.* San Diego, CA: Silver Dolphin Books, 2010.

Websites

Comets and Meteors: Shooting Stars
www.esa.int/esaKIDSen/SEM059WJD1E_OurUniverse_0.html
Read more about meteors and many other space topics.

Meteor Showers: Where, When, and How to Look for Them
planetary.org/explore/kids/activities/meteor_showers.html
Get tips about looking for meteor showers, and try other fun space activities.

INDEX